YOU AND YOUR WEIGHT

By Eileen Renders

Published by Eileen Renders

Author Eileen Renders

Bowker ISBN 979-8-218-96113-8

First edition

INTRODUCTION

My background and experience as a Nutritionist, health research freelance writer, and Certified Wellness Coach qualifies me write this book, as well as to share with you my own personal account of a successful weight management program.

Each chapter will introduce you to healthier lifestyle practices that will unlock new ways of approaching food along with the instituting of new lifestyle habits.

It is of most importance to preface all this new information that you will be taking in upon the pages you are about to read by saying that once the seed has been planted allow some time for the seed to grow. In other words; one new change at a time, and allow that change to become habitual before moving on to take on another change.

Success comes with planning and over a period of time in order for it to remain successful. Select those changes that are most comfortable to you initially, and then take on another change. Also, do not associate your degree of success with the scale. Often times, we may be holding excess water, maaybe from high sodium intake, for women (depending upon age) it could be that time of the month, there are a few other causes as well, such as a bit of constipation. Decide to measure your success by getting weighed once a month on the same date. Day to day weight usually will indeed fluctuate.

CHAPTERS

Chapter One

Hunger and Saiety

Much research and some philosophy surround the idea of being "over-weight" and obese. Some reserch for example suggests that some types of obesity are genetic, in that we inherit more, or less the type and number of fat cells that our parents have been give and pass on. That my be true to some degree, however what is true is that we are raised as children and young adults to eat what mom cooks up, what the rest of . the family also consumes on a daily basis. Some families, however consume more quantities of say fried foods, sweets and/or over-processed foods. We would then become accustomed to eating in that manner for the rest of our lives.

Perhaps only after being diagnosedd with a health disorder and being told by a medical doctor to lose weight, or for others possibly reaching that age when we find ourselves attracted to an individual of the opposite sex who may be an individual who demonstrates a sense of "fitness" and a desire for healthy foods might we take a personal inventory of ourselves.

However that works out for some of us, since you are here now reading this book title, you are expressing a desire for change. I can recall a Lighting Company as a child that promoted the Logo "Progress is Change". I rather liked that and it remains today in my memory.

At any rate, let us now begin to move forward and consider "Hunger and Saiety." Foremost it is safe to say that if we have been out and about and had a busy and active day, it is quite normal to become hungry. But, how does hunger evolve? What causes those hunger pangs most of us have experienced from time to time?

For most of us, hunger pangs are a normal response to the stomach being empty, and they are known as stomach contractions accompanied by the desire to eat.

For others, it could be a rare disorder know as an impaired MC4R pathway that is the root of the excess, or constant hunger causing obesity who are living with Bardet-Biedl Syndrome, or BBS. More information and how this disorder is diagnosed may be found at
https://rareobesity.com/pathophysiology

Again, for most of us hunger is a normal response to not having eaten for awhile, or not eating enough of food and nutrients. In fact, some research suggests that whenever we eat non-nutritious, excess sugary foods such as say doughnuts, our bod is not satisfied. It is signaling for nutrition, yet many will be more prone to have nother doughnut!

Eating healthy fresh foods on the other hand, is provided with the nutrients that will create a sense of energy and positivity.

As an individual with some level of expertise in nutrients, we would be wise then to keep in mind how deficiencies in the essential nutrients, enzymes and/or hormones can cause distress and lead to symptoms that need to be addressed. Just about everyone has heard the stories of Vitamin deficiencies aand symmptoms and health issues associated with these deficiencies. For example; a deficiencie in Vitamin-C can lead to depression, weakened blood vessels, immunity problems and more.

A deficiency in Vitamin-D in children leads to a disorder known as Rickets whereby growth is stunted, bones become softened, bow legs and other problems.

Without going deeper into the Vitamin deficiencies and their relationship to disease, let us just consider how important it is for us to chose foods that provide us nourishment, rather than giving in to a sugar addiction that leads to obesity and other digestive problems. The fact that sugar and artificial sweeteners are highly acidic should be enough for us to refrain from those types of food in excess.

What does a highly acidic diet mean to us? Highly acidic foods create a higher risk for certain types of cancers. Because wee are comprised of three-quarters composition in our body, we must maintain a healthy ph value as does the Swimming pool, or the Fish tank.

A healthier substitute for refined white sugar could be Monk fruit, or honey used in lower quantities and not too frequently.

It is good to begin to acquire a taste for salads, vegetables, and yes potatoes. Because meats are highly acidic as well, consider the alternatives, such as rice and beans, plant proteins, or fish.

Chapter Two

Fat/weight loss and Hormones

Researching hormones, we have learned (according to many scientific reports) that there are hormones that influence our appetite and there are hormones that signal the brain that our hunger has been satisfied.

In another chapter we will review which foods are most compatible with those hormones that will assist us in losing excess weight.

In this chapter however, we will take a look at these hormones that affect the appetite.

Amylin ~ Amylin works as a Satiety hormone. This hormone, Amylin has a unique pharmacology, physiology and therefore, Clinical Potential. Amylin in the literature in rodents and in humans on anylin malyin is a pancreatic b-cell hormone that produces effects in several different organ systems. In this review we learn thant Amylin is a 37-amino-acid peptide discovered 25 years ago and it activates specific receptors, which are multi-sub-unit G-protein-coupled receptor subtypes.

Amylin's primase.ary role is as a glucoregulatory hormone, and its n importnt regulator of energy metabolism in helth and disease. Other Amylin actions have been reported, such as on the Cardiovascular system and on the bone. Amylin acts primarily in the circumventicular organs of the central nervous system and functionally interacts with other metabolically active hormones such s cholecystokinin, leptin, and estradiol. The mylin-bsed peptide, pramlintide, is used clinically to treat type 1 and type 2 diabetes, Clinical studies in obesity have shown that Amylin agonists could also be useful for weight loss, especially in combination with other agents.

Affiliations PMID; 26071095 DOI; 10.1124/pr.115.010629

Debbie L Hay, Steve Chen, Thomas A Lutz, David G Parkes, Jonathan D Roth

Cholecystokinin (CCK) ~ Cholecystokinin, or CCK, is a hormone released by cells in the gut when eating meals. CCK dampens hunger by sending a signal to the brain that the body is satiated. After losing weight however, in lowering caloric intake, there may be a reduction in CCK that might affect hunger and lead to a weight regain.

Ghrelin ~ Ghrelin is a hunger hormone best known for its part in starting the feelings associated with hunger. Although Ghrelin levels are highest after someone has not eaten for a while, or just prior to eating a regular meal, such as breakfast, lunch and dinner.

It has been found that Ghrelin levels may increase after weight loss from reducing calories. Therefore, this hormone can also be associated with an increase of appetite and contribute to a regain of lost weight.

GLP-1 ~ Glucagon-like peptide-1, or GLP-1, This is a hormone that is made mainly in the gut, however might also be from the brain. GLP-1 is stimulated in response to eating food that are known to help with the feeling of being full, or satisfied. However, once again after losing weight by limiting caloric intake, GLP-1 levels may be reduced, thereby adding to increased appetite and leading to a weight regain.

Insulin ~ Insulin is a hormone made within the pancreas, responsible for allowing sugar to enter cells and be utilized as energy. Thus, without insulin, the body would surely be unable to fuel itself. Insulin assists the body in knowing when it is full, and therefore reduce the amount of calories consumed. But again, after losing weight in limiting caloric intake, the hormone Insulin may show a reduction in insulin levels, and that can add to increased hunger with a weight regain.

Leptin ~ Leptin is a hormone manufactured by one's fat cells throughout the body, and Leptin is released by fat cells, which conveys to the brain when one has eaten sufficiently. Leptin levels may be reduced after weight loss, and also add to increased hunger with a weight regain.

Peptide YY (PYY) ~ PYY signals the brain that the body is satisfied after eating. Yet again, PYY levels become reduced after weight loss, which can also lead to regaining weight.

Authors note: While these hormones are certainly necessary and provide benefit to the human organs and especially the digestive system, one might also see how with weight loss, they can also become sort of counter-productive such as in what is referred to as a re-bound effect. Therefore, one would be wise not to count on continued support for one's weight loss goals. Furthermore, in the scales of life, it is balance that helps to prevent an upset of weight.

In other words, it will be necessary to make a few positive changes in one's eating habits, lifestyle practices and in one's thinking before lasting effects will be noticed and can be sustained.

Always keeping in mind that one easy to achieve lasting change at a time is all that is required. Two relatively obvious studies have confirmed that fast weight loss is usually never maintained. This is probably due to the fact that the one who lost this weight faster than medically desisred was fasting, starving, or on a difficult to keep diet. Dieting is not the answer in maintaining a healthy weight loss because there are few people willing to remain on a "diet."

On the other hand, understanding how hig sodium, excess sugary foods and drinks have no nutritional value and caause weight gain for example, is a much better motivation for switching say to an iced tea drink with a bit of monkfruit as your sweetener.

Understanding often times, it is not how much you eat in one day, as it could be that it is the type of unhealthy foods you are eating on a regular basis.

Another example is how often some people, possibly in aerbs bind for time, may include a can, or a bag of frozen vegetables with a huge piece of red meat. Red meat is highly acidic and often contains much fat. Vegetables however, have various delicious ways of being heated and/or cooked. Such as sautee'd with a variety of other vegetables, adding a bit of herbs, such as Paprika, or Basil, cooking wine, mushrooms, onions, garlic, or parmasean cheese.

So indeed, it is a good idea to change the way we view the fods we eat. This idea brings to mind a saying that certainly clarifies that there are two ways of doing and/or saying something. How many times have we ourselves been offended, not in what someone has said to us, but in the manner, or tone in which it was said?

This is sort of how some of us may get in a cooking rut in thinking I will open up a can of string beans, rather than a string bean casserole, or another similar creative way. If there is no time, with working and/or raising a family, we can always step up to the plate (excuse the pun) and experiment with creativity in the kitchen for ourselves and for our family. It is a great way of showing love and teaching our children.

Chapter Three

Foods Containing Food Hormones

Foods that help to burn fat

Avacados	Bananas	Beans
Berries	Broccoli	Coconut oil
Eggs	Grapefruit	Green tea
green leafy vegetables		hot peppers
Legumes	Olive oil	Peanut butter
Salmon	Soybeans	Walnuts
Whey protein	Whole grains	Yogurt

Foods that provide little or No Nutrition and

Contribute to weight gain

Sugary foods, such as cakes, cookies, sodas, ice cream. candy, and/or high Sodium, oily and fried foods such as potato chips, french fries and highly processed foods.

Highly processed foods contain food additives of which many can cause health issues, and a good example is at least one of the sugar substitutes. Many of your highly processed foods contain food dyes, especially in candies. In some instances thes dyes can contribute to health and/or cognitive conditions, especially in children.

For those desiring to know more about processed foods and understanding Ingredient labels on various foods, I recommend a book that I authored some years back titled FOOD ADDITIVES, NUTRIENTS AND SUPPLEMENTS A TO Z. Available at http://www.Amazon.com

In my lecturing, I am often approached and asked "What are processed foods." Without going into an in-depth Class on the subject, my reply is simple; Processed foods would be anything sold in a box, a can, or a bag. While many, many foods are processed, there are huge amounts of products that I like to refer to as "overly processed." Again, those interested in lnowing more, especially when it comes to being an example to their children

Might want to consider purchasing the above referenced book to keep around the house as a reference guide and something to refer to occasionally.

Foods that are usually able to be consumed in reasonable aamount would be home-made soups (low sodium), Salads, Vegetable entrees, and whole grains.

Chapter Four

Exercise

**Important note

We are all different individuals with different health issues, at different stages of life and of course, diagnosed with very different types of disorders, many of which require different types of medications. Therefore, one must always meet with their doctor to discuss safe types of exercise recommended with specific instructions to determine time alotment for such exercise and limitations regarding heart rate and etc.

The following information is taken from the Mayo Clinic regarding their findings with reference to a regular routine of exercise and the benefits associated with exercise.

Exercise prevents or manages many health problems, including; Stroke

Metbolic syndrome

High blood pressure

Type 2 diabetes

Depression

Anxiety

Many types of cancer

Arthritis

Falls

With all of the above benefits, plus its known ability to improve mood, energy and sleep, regular exercise is always recommended for everyone.

And also helps to improve cognitive function and help lower the risk of death from all causes.

A couple of causes that increase the risk for obesity include depression aand low self-esteem.

Regular exercise improves brain helth, which may aleviate depression and reduce the risk of disease. And exercise strengthens bones thereby motivating energy, and is a boost to the immune system.

Avoiding outside weather extremes associated with Seasons and climate, a suitable type of exercise for many seniors, or those with disabilities may be on a comfortable indoor bike, or simply walking. Discuss with your doctor.

Actually, exercise is the best way to burn calories, and produce energy. It has so many benefits such as lowering cholesterol, creating a healthy digestive system, releasing positive neurons, enzymes and more. All of which works to assist us in maintaining a healthy weight, along with a positive attitude. To take it a step further, we will sleep better, and awake with a clear head and energy to keep us fueled throughout the day!

When we work to create positivity by making positive healthy food choices, it soon becomes automatic, in other words, with choosing we know what we want to eat because we have realized the great gains and benefits of eating for life, rather than living to eat!

We soon find ourselves becoming positive example to our children, mentors to our friends, as they will want to know your secrets!

Chapter Five

Intermittent Fasting

This type of weight management appears to have become a popular and somewhat successful method for successful weight management. Because it allows for your basic three meal a day plan, it can be quite adaptable. Provided of course, meal planning is not a hurried grab for what is available types of food tht may not provide much nutrition, or eaten in excessive amounts.

It is worth reminding one's self that after consuming food, it does take the brain aa few minutes to interpret the sensation that one's hunger has been satisfied.

In the next few pages we will discuss some of the possible side-effects associated with intermittent fasting or IF for a period of 16 hours. This would be especially true for anyone diagnosed with diabetes, especially Type 1 diabetes.

Personally, I have always practiced intermittent fasting in that after my dinner, I refrined from eating until breakfast the next morning, and not necessarily for weight reasons. However, my fasting is between 10 to 12 hours, rather than 16 hours, which I believe would not be resonable.

The article in WOMEN'S HEALTH Magazine is titled "1-Intermittent Fasting Side Effects That Might Mean It's Not A Great Fit For You." By Sarah Bradley, Srah Fellbin and Ashley Martens and published March, 2023.

In condensed style, this article relates that an Intermittent Fasting program has been linked to not only a desired weight loss, but less bodily inflammation and better concentration. Alyssa Koens RD states the importance to determine which type of IF works best for you as there is a shorter version verses the longer fasting version, and that might mean fewer days and/or shorter fasting hours each day.

Audrey Fleck, RDN says that even for the 16:8 method, which is one of the more popular methods, there are those who may not be able to adapt to the schedule. Because there currently are no official guidelines for exactly what the IF routine should be, it is up to each individual to discover which routine works best for them. Intermittent Fasting is still very much in the research stage, however there are some very promising findings to date.

   It cannot be over-emphasized that should some experience side-effects from this type of Fasting, that is exactly why it is necessary for your doctor to educate the individual on which side-effects are not serious, and possibly temporary, or perhaps offer an anedote for one's discomfort. This of course, being separated from a possible more serious side-effect. *Because of one's blood sugar readings, this is imperative for those with diabetes.

   Personally, from my own point of view (and I am not a diabetic), but I am Celiac and have my gall bladder removed and have occasional GERD (acid-reflux). And I prevent any digestive discomfort by taking Digestive enzymes that contain both prebiotica and probiotics everyday.

Symptoms that may present include; These first Five Symptoms are found mostly to be temporary and include how to aleviate them.

1. **Hangriness** ~ This is a feeling as described within this article as a feeling both of irritability and discomfort that comes from not being able to eat when your body is telling you it is hungry.

2. **Fatigue or Brain Fog** ~ Brain fog can be described as waking up groggy as though you have not had enough sleep, for making mistakes as though you are in a fog. This could be an alert that the foods you are eating during non-fasting hours are not providing the required nutrients to provide the fuel to run your body efficiently, or perhaps your diet needs modification. Although you can eat what you want on the IF diet, you must still ensure that your body is getting the food types that will fuel your body and make it feel healthy and strons, says Koens.

3. **Low Blood Sugar** ~ If you're having persistent nausea, headaches, or dizziness during IF, that is a red flag that indicates the diet may be throwing your blood sugar out of whack. Diabetics should avoid any kind of Fasting diet. IF or Itermittent Fasting can cause you to become

hypoglycemic, a dangerous condition for anyone with insulin or thyroid problems.

4. **Constipation** ~ Constipation usually is triggered by not drinking a sufficient amount of water, and/or by not taking in sufficient amounts of vitamins, proteins and fiber. It is advised not to try and force it, but perhaps taking a mild stool softener and drinking more water and ensuring you are eating foods containing all the nutrients required to maintain a healthy colon.

Long-Term Intermittent Fasting Side Effects

1. **Food Obsessions** ~ As stated in Women's Health article. Any kind of restrictive diet can affect your relationship with food, as stated by Koens. While some individuals like a restrictive type of diet, others will find themselves focusing too much on when to eat, how many calories and what they probably should not be eating. Spending too much time dwelling on food can ead to a disorder called orthorexia. Having orthorexia means you focus so much on "correct", or "healthful" eating that it actually

has a detrimental effect on your overall well-being, this ccording to The National Eating Disorders Association. In 2022 a study published in the journal *Eating Disorders* found men and women who follow IF score significantly higher in Eating Disorder Examination Questionnaire compared to those who are eating a normal diet. "You want to focus on forming a healthy, positive relationship with food" says Koens.

Note from Book Author: Because you will be Fasting, it is helpful to maintain the idea that you *can* basically eat the foods you prefer, however without over-eating and keeping a safe distance from Junk foods. Those being Sweets, Fried foods, and overly processed foods.

2. **Hair Loss** ~ Koens cautions that yes, hair loss can occur on a Fasting diet, especially one lacking essential protein, B-Vitamins and essential nutrients. The article adds a word from Goodstadt who notes that although some studies suggest calorie restriction can lead to hair loss, more research needs to be done in order to fully demonstrate this relationship.

3. **Changes in Your Menstrual Cycle** ~ Here is another side-effect of sudden weight loss (which can be a result of Intermittent Fasting); Women who lose a dramatic amount of weight or are consistently not getting enough calories every day might find their menstrual cycles slow down or even stop completely, as noted in a 2021 study published in *Experimental Gerontology*, as well as a 2019 study published in the journal *Obesity*. If your period has stopped and you think it is attributed to fasting, stop fasting and speak with your gynecologist right away.

Book Author note: It is expected during a Fast to eat less food, however the risk for these side-effects may be more, or less associated with continuing to eat the wrong foods without nutritional value, as it is with beginning to eat a bit less food per day. See your doctor.

4. **Unhealthy Diet** ~ Charlie Seltzer, MD states that even if Intermittent Fasting does not trigger a serious disorder like orthorexia, it could still bring about some pretty unhealthy eating habits. In addition to not getting the

proper nutrition as far as necessary nutrients, you could also find yourself making a mess in nutritious choices during non-fasting hours. And the main concern is setting off binge-eating behavior because you are so hungry you're eating 5,000 calories (and going way over your daily amount of calories. Charlie Seltzer MD is a weight-loss physician and certified personal trainer, previously with Women's health Magazine.

5. **Sleep Disturbances** ~ Many people report improved sleep patterns while doing IF, possibly due to the way IF helps curb late-night snacking habits, and in turn, an inability to fall asleep because your stomach is busy digesting that 10 p.m. snacking, Koen says.

However, there is some research pointing to the opposite effect. A 2018 review in the journal *Nature and Science of Sleep* shows that diurnal intermittent fasting (meaning daytime fasting) causes a *decrease* in rapid-eye movement (REM) sleep. Getting enough REM sleep has been linked to all kinds of benefits, including better memory, cognitive processing and concentration, so you definitely don't want to miss out on quality shuteye.

If you can't fall asleep or stay asleep after you have started an IF eating plan, again, take a break from the diet and talk to a pro to make sure you are not hurting your health.

Note by Book Author: While the above notes mention diurnal fasting, or daytime fasting, I believe that after dinner, the evening meal, or night-time fasting may not in most people cause poor sleeping habits, and that is to be determined.

6. **Mood Changes** ~ The article notes in its finality that it would be weird if you did not experience any moodiness or "ahem" *hangriness* during IF, at lest in the beginning. And while some people feel a serious boost of energy or motivation once they have adjusted to fasting, it's iportant to remember that it is still a restrictive diet. Feeling obligated to follow t could have negative effects on your mood, especially if you're becoming isolate from friends or family members due to your diet restrictions.

Final note by book author: My final word would be to undertake all that you endeavor with a positive attitude while being cautious. If it helps for the first week or two, write down what your are eating with Caloric amount just to examine how many calories you are consuming, and whether or not, you are consuming unhealthy foods.

Chapter Six

Lifetime Changes

Lifetime changes require a desire for change and a commitment to those desired changes. Therefore, should we one day discover that our last couple of days certainly were far from upholding that commitment, it is not a failure. We can just pick ourselves up and renew that commitment by beginning anew one more time!

We are all human and subject to little failures here and there, yet that does not mean we will not prevail.

What exactly are lifetime changes you may ask. Lifetime changes are just what the term implies, a lifetime of keeping our eye on our objective and renewing our commitment whenever that is necessary. In this scenario, our lifetime changes within these pages are relative to our health, protecting and nurturing healthy habits that will increase our productivity, immune system, enjoyment and longevity.

It is reasonable then, to expect that we must create healthy habits, chosing nutritional foods that will provide essential nutrients, antioxidants that assist our immune system to remain effictive so that we might avoid disease, enjoy the energy that we are creating within our body, and in turn expand our productivity and increase our chances of living a long healthy life.

If it sounds too good to be true, evidence suggests that in fact, it is true. Recently, we lost one of America's icons, Tony Bennet passed away on July 21, 2023 at the age of 96 years of age. And, I might add continued to utilize his talent as a singer up until he was 94 years of age and was diagnosed with Alzeheimers disease.

As I write these pages, I am writing my fourth book in two years, and will be 84 years of age this November of the year 2023. Yet I exercise 5 days a week, drive a car, cook for my husband and myself 7 days a week because we want and appreciate healthy food. I'm smiling now as I recall when we were 50 years of age some 24 years ago, we quit smoking cigrettes. It was difficult as it is an addiction. Once we were comfortable being non-smokers, we realized that we could not be around anyone who was smoking. It totally made us uncomfortable and did not like the smell of it.

The same thing can be said when we gave up the Salt, everything tasted, well let's say everything had no taste, it was bland. Soon we began to taste the foods we were eating, rather than the Salt content, that was a discovery! At the same time, I began cooking with garlic, herbs and spices, sauteeing our vegetables and that made it so easy to then reduce the red meat in our diet and eat more fish, plant protein and realize the benefits of a healthy diet.

Let me say howeever, these lifestyle changes that I made (and included my husband) truly have made a difference, and have been accomplished not in a month, or a year, but in several years. My doctors tell me today (who are in their 60's) that they want to be like me when they reach my age. That is not only a compliment, but also a confirmation that I have as they say "been doing somethng right."

Truly I tell you, of my virtues I believe I am sharing those that often come with age, namely wisdom. Still, I must admit to my weaknesses and faults. One fault I can assure you is not that of patience, so the changes in my life were not easy to come by, yet my desire to live a healthy life was stronger. Determination *is* something that I have a bit of.

Perhaps choosing the healthy lifetime changes that you feel comfortable about and confident that you can accomplish is a good place to begin. Whenever we expect too much of ourselves, and all too soon, we may simply be listening to that negative side of ourselves that is trying to thwart our effort.

If you find yourself having problems that you are unsure of how to overcome, join a group of others with the same goals for support.

There is a strong warning that deserves its place on this page. For after having said join a group, I whole heartedly caution you *not* to join a support group that has a different goal than your own. In other words, there will be those who wish to lose weight at any cost for the sake of vanity. Continue on down the road seeking a support group wanting to take it a bit slower, with a goal of becoming healthier, more energetic, preventing disease and seeking a longer life. Maybe taking a bold step forward and starting your own local group.

The new positive attitude that develops within you can open the door to a world of new possibilities, such as helpng others.

We only go around once, one life to live! Live it to the fullest of your capabilities, if you have children, lead them and guide them to also make the most of their God given life!

A support group should have leadership, support and available information, meet regularly and have the same goals. A good example is Alcoholics Anonymous. Their one goal is to remain sober no matter what!

Before we move on, let me say that balance is important to us in more ways than one. There must be room in our lives for mistakes, correction and a return to balance. Rarely is one individual, or one circumstance either all right, or all wrong. The world is not all black and white. Stop and smell the roses, be kind to yourself, love yourself and love others, for this is a good place to be.

Think of our children. Babies must learn to crawl before they walk, and walk before they run. It is a matter of learning, and trusting one's self, and takes time.

Chapter Seven

The New You

Now that you have initiated your customized weight loss program with your doctor's approval and you are beginning to realize some success, how do you proceed?

Well, the good news is that you should take one day a week and allow yourself that big slice of cheesecake, or a side of french fries. Pat yourself on the back because we never have to say *never* to ourselves. And we have received much more than we have given up. We have learned that we really can live without that slice of cheesecake, we are achievers, we look better, we are beginning to feel energized and can happily maintain a positive attitude as we go forward. Avoid the pitfalls of vanity. Vanity takes us often down a non-productive road where focus remains on ourselves and our looks, rather than on the next challenge, our next goal and who we are. That is, what we are made of.

Life itself I have been known to comment about in the past by saying "Life is not who we are, or what we were, but who we are becoming"!

Let it be said once more that vanity prevents us from finding new challenges and goals, and keeps us focused on ourselves. Small world indeed!

Imagine the connotations of achieving your goal of finding and maintaining the magic number that fits your desired weight goal. And now that you have succeeded, you can now continue to find open doors that will reveal countless opportunities to further express who you really are, and that you are a serious competitor in the scheme of life.

Congratulate yourself and begin to plan how you move forward, spend some time going inward and pondering exactly what it was that motivated you. And just as importantly, examine your conscience as to what it is you believe has held you back from achieving your goals for such a time. For *those* are the beliefs that you now want to change.

It cannot be stressed enough, the new you is not all about looks, although you are looking your best! More than that, we are able to take what we have learned, and what I am referring to here is the positive choices and attitude that will remain with you for the rest of your life!

Although all of us are not on this life permanently, we can feel proud that we met the challenge of obesity, low-self esteem, healthy issues, and we have conquered. Moreover, as we gradually move through the decades, and on into old age, we are more likely to enjoy many of the things in life that we have most enjoyed such as; Driving, travel, cooking, dining out with friends and family, and many of our hobbies. Hopefully will still be able to exercise a bit. Elderly people can often ride a Stationary bike, use some light weight hand weights, walk, or swim.

Chapter Eight

This Is Not A Diet Book

In turning your thoughts from the idea of *dieting* in exchange for the concept of *chosing healthy foods* you have changed not only how you are looking, but also how your feel and in many ways, how you think.

The very idea of a diet suggests that it is temporary, until one has reached the desired weight loss that is needed. Also, the concept of dieting indicates (s described in the dictionary) that it is necessary to restrict onself to small amounts or special kinds of food in order to lose weight. And needless to say, that is not something that anyone wants to adopt as a lifetime process.

Therefore, losing weight, gaining energy, and staying healthy is an altogether different concept from the idea of *dieting.*

For example; When we want and are willing to understand our nutritional needs, changing how we eat becomes secondary, and we develop a taste for healthy foods. Most often, we can eat as much as it takes to satisy our energy needs without gaining weight. Plus, we are using this energy to continue on with our newly established exercise plan. Be it 4 or 5 days a week, it becomes a habit much like brushing our teeth in the morning. Too, we have the fun of a little reward in that we now can enjoy shopping for a few new pieces of clothing. We become more outgoing, making new friends, and developing a calendar of invitations, things to do.

Therefore, who would want to exchange that for sitting alone in our car munching on french fries, or going home with a bag of doughnuts? Not a chance!

It is a new way of life. Everything in life requires an adjustment such as going from single to married, going from maan and wife to having a family when a child is born.

Always remember, the more time you spend on becoming the healthier you, perhaps the more time you are adding to your life!

Chapter Nine

A Few Favorite Healthy Recipes

Turkey Sausage, Yellow Squash and Idaho potatoes

All in One big Electric Skillet

Ingredients

Precooked Turkey sausages (amount depending upon size of diners).

2 to 3 large fresh yellow Squash

Precooked Idaho potatoes

Ms. Dash (Lemon pepper)

*optional Small to medium sliced onion

½ tsp. fresh garlic

Sprinkle of parsley

Instructions

In a large Electric skillet or a large size Frying pan add the peeled and sliced yellow squash and Olive oil to the pan and cook on medium heat for approximately 4 to 5 minutes until they appear to have slightly softened.

Add garlic, parsley and onion and cook for another minute or so lprior to adding cooked potatoes and sausages.

Continue cooking until sausage and potatoes are slightly browned

Serve and enjoy!

Crispy Fried Egg Plant With Soy Crumbles

Ingredients

1 Medium size Eggplant

Bread crumbs

Olive oil 2-3 Tablespoons

One and a half cups of frozen Soy crumbles

Half a cup of cherry tomatoes

One stalk of celery diced

Half teaspoon of crushed garlic

1 to 1 ½ cups of Low-Sodium marinara sauce

Sprinkle of Parmasean cheese

Served with either a side Salad, or another vegetable of choice

Instructions

Utilizing 2 large Fry pans

Peel and slice eggplant and dip into a dish with one egg and a few tablespoons of milk, dip into breading

Place into a medium hot fry pan with oil. On low to medium heat, adding more oil as necessary to avoid drying out, and or stick to the pan.

Turning when each side has reached a light to medium brown, And adding more slices to Fry pan as deemed ideal amount for serving.

In another Fry pan add 2 table spoons of oil (preferably Extra Virgin Olive oil). On low to medium heat, add Soy crumbles, the sliced onion and cherry tomatoes.

Cook on low to medium heat for about 5 minutes.

Add one cup of Marinara sauce and combine

*Optional ~ Add 1/3 cup of Cooking wine

When full warmed, turn burner off and let rest for 5 minutes

Prior to Serving add Sprinkles of Parmasean cheese.

When sufficient egg plant sliced have been cooked, place on a Serving dish. Then add ½ cup of remaining Mrinara sauce to the fry pan and warm before pouring over the cooked eggplant.

Ready for Serving with optional Salad or another vegetable of choice!

Coconut Chicken and Red skinned potatoes

Ingredients

2- fresh chicken breasts

1 stalk of chopped celery

1 Talblspoon of crushed bacon

½ teaspoon of celery

4 medium sized red skin potatoes pre-boiled

Approximately 6 ounces of canned coconut milk

½ can of corn

Directions

Slice chicken breasts into 3 to 4 inch sections and cook in olive oil for approximately 8 minutes on each side.

Add remaining ingredients ~ except for Coconut milk

On medium heat and combine ingredients for about 5 minutees, adding olive oil if necessary, or a spritz or two of water or Sherry Cooking wine.

Finally, add Coconut milk and remain on stove on low heat for another 5 minutes or so before serving.

Warmed buns or crusty bread go well with this dish for dipping.

Tilapia or Flounder Entrée

Ingredients

3 to 4 large Slices of either fish

Beaten egg dip and plate for breadding

A tablespoon of Lemon juice

One-halp tablespoon of Old Bay Seasoning

Instructions

In a large Frying pan and two tablespoons of Extra virgin Olive oil

Add breaded flounder and top with Lemon juice and Old Bay Seasoning

Cook each side for approximately 5 minutes until a Light golden brown

*Optional Top with a half tablespoon of Blue cheese Salad dressing

Side dish While fish is frying, you may consider opening a frozen bag of vegetable pasta in another pan and heating according to directions, about Six minutes

Broiled Shrimp

Ingredients

Depending upon how many will be partaking

20 frozen peeled, or fresh medium to large sized Shrimp

Herbs and Spices

In a Small bowl for mixing, add the following for dusting Shrimp;

¾ tablespoon of Old Bay Seasoning

*Optional   ½ teaspoon of Jalopen powder

¼ teaspoon of Paprike

½ teaspoon of Garlic powder

½ tablespoon of Oregano

1/3 cup of oil

Mix together all of the spices and herbs with the oil

Instructions

Prepare oven for Broiling

On a <u>lined</u> shallow pan add single file, Shrimp that has been thoroughly dipped into above mixturer.

Note To save oven from spills, either line bottom of oven, or ensure that the broiling pan will not spill over and/or leak

Cook Shrimp for 3 to 4 minutes on both sides.

*Optional a prepared personal small dish containing a dipping sauce is a good idea.

This dish will go well with red skinned potatoes or oven baked french fries and a vegetable of your choice, such as corn.

Ham And Apple Potatoes

Ingredients

3 to 4 Slices of Low Sodium ham from your deli, cut for Pan heating. (Boar's Head is great if you Shop at Publix).

1 teaspoon of grainy mustard

4 to 6 boiled Idaho potatoes for mashing

1 large apple

1 Tablespoon of Butter and 1/3 cup of milk for whipping potatoes

¼ teaspoon of Salt for potatoes

½ teaspoon of Basil

Preecooked fresh Brussell Sprouts

Directions

In a medium size pot, boil potatoes,add peeled diced apple 10 minutes before potatoes are ready for mashing.

Add butter, milk and Basal before mashing

In a fry pan add the ham slices and lightly cover with the grainy mustard.

Cook ham slices about 5 inutes each side until lightly browned.

On a back burner cook your Brussell Sprouts

Ready to Serve!

A side Salad, or cole Slaw would go well with this dish!

Half-Homemade Lentil Soup

Ingredients

2 Cans of Low sodium Lentil Soup (Progresso makes a low sodium Lentil Soup)

2-3 Leeks Fryied up in 1-2 Tablespoons of Extra Virgin Olive oil until Lightly browned.

3 to 4 boiled, cut up Idaho potatoes

I Tablespoon of Parmasean cheese

*Optional ¼ cup of Cooking Sherry

Precooked potatoes

Pre fried Leeks

Open up 2 Cans of Low-sodium Lentil Soup and heat on medium in a large Pot.

Add the rest of the ingredients and continue cooking onn low heat for 5 to 6 minutes

Sprinkle with Parmasean ppwdered cheese and serve with a slice of Crusty bread

White Meat Lump Crab

Ingredients

White Lump fresh Crab meat – amount depending upon how many Servings necessary

Butter

Fresh Garlic

Dash of Oregano

¼ teaspoon of Old Bay Seasoning

Instructions

In a Medium sized bowl empty fresh lump white Crab meat

Add 2 to 3 Tablespoons of softened Butter

½ Tablespoon of fresh garlic

Dash of Oregano

¼ teaspoon of Old Bay Seasoning

Combine contents gently until blended

In a Medium Size Frypan, turn heat to Medium

Add the seasoned pieces of Crab meat and sautee' on each side for 2 to 3 minutes

Serving Suggestions

Take a half of a plain bagel and slice in half again

Take the thin ¼ of the bagel and lightly toast

On a Serving plate add the toasted ¼ of bagel and top with the Seasoned Crab meat – A side of Baked French fries or a favorite Side dish will go well

Chapter Ten

Quick and Healthy Snack Ideas

When hunger truly strikes, maybe because you did not supply sufficient energy to your body due to an extra busy day, or scheduled appointments, consider the following ideas, and ensure that these foods are always available for such times.

Low sugar, high fiber cereal

Yogurt

Eggs

A handful of low sodium healthy nuts, such as Almonds, Walnuts or Cashews

Fruit

A Salad

Dried fruit

Left over homemde soup

Shrimp Cocktail and a piece of crusty bread

Almond butter Sandwich with low sugar Jelly (rather that peanut butter).

Left over potatoes from previous evening meal. Sautee' in a pan with onions, peppers, corn.

Grab a scrubbed Idaho potato and microwave it, And a shake of garlic and a bit of butter.

We all know that pie, cake, or cookies adds no nutrition and is only a temporary relief from real hunger.

Chapter Eleven

Healthier Alternative Ingredient Choices

Rather than	Instead Choose
Sugar	Monk fruit, natural honey
Salt	Ms. Dash lemon/pepper
Butter	Ghee, plant based butter
Oil for frying	Broiling or Baking
White flour pasta	Lentil mix pasta flour
Sweetened iced tea	Unsweetened Iced with Lemonade (half and half)
White potatoes	Sweet potatoes, or red skin
Sweetened cereaals	Oatmeal
Out to dinner	
Highly sweetened Liquors	Dark red wine
White bread	Whole grain breads and rolls

| Ice cream | Frozen yogurt, or a Sundae |
| | with Fresh fruits, "Light" whipped cream and Walnuts |

** Hitting the Stores soon, a plant type of Ice Cream based on Oatmeal, tasty by all studies and standards

Doughnuts	Slice of lightly toasted whole
grain	
	Bread with a pat of Cake Icing
Whole Milk	1% Milk
Sodas	Fruit Water
Deep Fryer	Air Fryer
Candy	Dried sweetened Cherries and Cranberries
Chocolate	Cocoa is considered the most Pure and natural, without other Ingredients added

High fiber, low Carbohydrate Food Choices

Almonds ¼ cup contains 8 grams of Carbohydrates and 4.5 grams of fiber, a very heart healthy food

Apples 1 medium apple has 25 grams of carbohydrate and 4.5 grams of fiber

Artichoke hearts ½ cup (Stove top boiled) contains 9.5 grams of Carbohydrate and 4.8 grams of fiber. Some research suggests this food is linked to a loweer risk of cancer

Asparagus 1 cup provides 5 grams of Carbohydrates and 2.8 grams of fiber

Avocado Approximately 1/3 of a medium Avocado provides 5 grams of Carbohydrte and 4 grams of fiber

Bell peppers 1 cup equals 4.3 Carbs and 1.6 grams of fiber

Blackberries 1 cup has 14 grams of Carbohydrate and 8 grams of fiber

Blueberries 1 cup has 21.5 grams of Crbohydrate with 4 grams of fiber

Broccoli   1 cup 5 grams of Carbohydrate, 2.5 grams of fiber

Brussels sprouts   Just a half dozen sprouts contain 8 grams of Carbohydrate and 3 grams of fiber

Cauliflower 1 cup provides 5 grams of Carbohydrates and 2.1 grams of fiber

Collard greens   1 cup is 4 grams of Carbohydrates and 4 grams of fiber

Eggplant   1 cup is 5 grams of Carbohydrate and 2.5 grams of fiber

Flax seed 1 Tablespoon contains 3 Carbs and 2.8 grams of fiber, and grea for adding cereal, satisfies hunger and helps to prevent Constipation

Frozen Spinach   1 cup provides 4 grams of Carbohydrates and 3 grams of fiber

Green peas 1 cup is 21 Carbohydrates and 7 grams of fiber

Kimchi   1 cup is 4 grams of Carbohydrates and 2.4 grams of fiber. This East Asian food has also other health benefits for the gastrointestinal tract in that it is a fermented food and a source of prebiotics and probiotics

Lentils ½ cup of cooked Lentils contain 20 grams of Carbohydrates and 8 grams of fiber. *See my recipe for Lentil soup, which requires no soaking or cooking under Recipes.

Macadamia nuts 1 cup 19 grams 1nd 12 grams of fiber

Pears 1 medium pear contains 27 Carbohydrates and 6 grams of fiber

Pumpkin seeds ½ cup provides 15 grams of Carbohydrate and a huge 12 grams of fiber, and is beneficial to the arteries

Radishes 1 cup is 4 grams of Crbohydrate with 2 grams of fiber

Raspberries 1 cup contains 14 grams of Carbohydrate and a whopping 8 grams of fiber

Walnuts 1 cup 11 grams of carbohydrate, 5 grams of fiber, and is high in anti-inflammatory ingredients, such as Alpha-linolenic acids. Great for blood vessels.

Winter Squash 1 cup provides 10 grams of Carbohydrates and 2.2 grams of fiber

Zucchini I cup provides 3.5 grams of Carbohydrates and 1.1 grams of fiber

Fiber is filling, help to satisy hunger and provides many vitamins and nutrients. Another benefit is how fiberlowers the bad cholesterol.

Chapter Twelve

Tips And Reminders For Mintaining Your New Ideal Weight

~ The largest meal of the day is best to be eaten mid-day so as not to go to bed with a full stomache with undidgested food.

~ Exercise must be consistent 4 to 5 days a week, perhaps count on taking the weekends off. If you miss a day, then add one weekend day to compensate.

~ Intermittent Fasting is a good way to eliminate late night snacking and all those extra calories. Eat three nutritious meals a day, and after dinner a fasting of 10 to 12 hours is beneficial.

***Intermittent Fasting is not advised for those with Diabetes as this could cause serious consequences.

~ When craving something sweet, consider your fvorite fruit cut up into a bowl, adding a handful of nuts for fiber and top with a Light spray of canned whipped cream topping.

~ Sweetened Soda drinks are not advisable at all, opt for water with lemon and you will quickly develop a taste for what the body requires. Our bodies remember, are comprised of ¾ water and it is important to our health (and even the skin) to stay hydrated.

~ If you go to bed occasionally and find that you aare still hungry after having had your three meals, a brief feeling of hunger will not cause any physical problems, let it happen. Or go to the kitchen and have a piece of fruit without grabbing the first thing you see.

~ Excess Sodium causes water retention and requires extra work on the circulatory system and raises the risk for high blood pressure.

~ Red meat is highly acidic and raises our risk for certain types of cancer. Our body is three-quarters water composition, and not unlike a Swimming pool, or Fish Tank, requires maintaining a good Ph balance. It is best not to eat red meat everyday, and when we do eat red meat, a serving is about the size of the palm of your hand.

Alternative to red meat include: Fish, rice and beans, or rice and corn, plant protein, eggs, and more.

~ By now you should have become familiar with ingredient labels and are aware of Sugar, Sodium, Fiber and Caloric content. Making it easier to compare similar brands, or remove some of the unhealthy types of foods that you may have chosen previously.

~ Remember to cultivate your culinary abilities by experimenting creativity in the kitchen.

~ Make it a Shopping habit to plan each main day meal while at the Market, seek out healthy snacks such as a good peanut and fruit option, or crackers with low sugar jelly. If you do not buy doughnuts and candy, you will not be tempted to snack on them.

Raisins, Cranberries, Banannas with a dash of Hersheys chocolate syrup (about ½ teaspoon) and a few nuts will satisfy and provide many nutrients and fiber.

~ Regularity and consistency is what builds habits that keep us fueled and energetic with a desire to enjoy what we have conquered and maintain a cool sense of control.

~ Reward yourself now that you have lost weight and buy yourself a couple new outfits, it will help to keep you on track as well.

~ Weighing in should only be done once or twice a month wearing similar clothing and at the same time of day. Weighing one's self every day is deceiving as our weight fluctuates according to when we have had our last meal, how much water we may be retaining and etc. This type of practice also causes the risk of placing too much emphasis on our weight (rather than selecting healthy food types, along with leading an active life), and might cause one to become a bit depressed thinking perhaps "I am not succeeding" when in fact, one maay be simply hold excess water due to consumption of too much sodium.

~ In order to remain hydrated, remember to take a bottle of water with you when out and about. Some research suggests that the brain's most significnt goal is to maintain energy in order to preserve life. Even more important than fluid intake, or hydration. However, in the midst of dehydration the body can result in feelings or symptoms of hunger, although what the body actually requires is water! Always remember our body is comprised of ¾ of water.

In fact, because the stomach growls is not proof positive that the body is asking for food. Should that sense of hunger be accompanied by a headache, dizziness, or nausea, it very well be that the stomache is actually signaling for hydration.

~ Also, in an attempt to lose weight, or maintain weight lost, we need to drink plenty of water and we will not be bothered by "false hunger."

~ FOOD SHOPPING Most of us in our lives have at one time or another purchased something only to later realize that it was money unnecessrily spent. Really, does not fit well, adds little to our lifestyle, or whatever.

Food Shopping is just as important. Before heading to the Supermarket, it may be a good idea to plan ahead for the weekly meals as our priority for the week, next might be essentials such as dry goods, or from the phaarmaceutical area. Impulse buying can often lead to going home with a week's, or a month's worth of non-nutritional treats, and without a plan for a healthy meal each day throughout the week.

Chapter Thirteen

Avoiding the Moody Munchies and Other causes of Obesity!

Anxiety~ Anxiety is quite often the feeling of fear, or worry about happenings, or attitudes and beliefs in others, all of which we have no control. AA or Alcoholics Anonymous has a Logo, which goes like this; "God grant me the serenity to change the things I can change, accept the things I cannot change, and the wisdom to know the difference." It is quite comforting to remind ourselves as many times as necessary that we cannot change others, the only thing we can change is ourselves.

Anxiety can keep us awaake at night, loss of energy, a feeling of tiredness upon waking in the morning, and not feeling refreshed, or ready for a new day!

Often time, whenever some of us lay awake at night and cannot sleep, we might get up and go raid the refrigerator.

Again, Anxiety can also arise from a genetic nerve center problem, or some sort of vitamin and.or nutritional deficiency, especially when we are not eating healthy. And sleep comes more readily when we have spent our day in being active and expending energy. *But remember,* Spending energy means that we first need to consume foods that contain energy!

Depression ~ Negative feelings and emotions express themselves in ways we all can relate to, such as low energy, futileness, or in feelings of failure. Depending how deep these emotions hang around and the intensity of these feelings very much should help individuals when to seek medocal and/or psychological intervention. Depression is a well known emotional imbalance in many individuals who received no intervention, and emotions progressed to the point that many have taken their own life.

Genes ~ * Mentioned in Chapter One

Isolation ~ Sometimes isolation can occur, and often does in the elderly. Therefore, this often happens when an individual becomes physically, or mentally impaired and are placed into a Nursing home. Often, they do not adjust in their new surroundings, they may be uninterested in making new friends, or learning new hobbies. This can often result in also becoming dis-interested in food, keeping to themselves and not thriving!

As human beings we are meant to interact, to share and to enjoy companionship of others to enjoy the diversity of hearing others share, rather than beingn left alone with our thoughts, mostly filled with the past! Living for today is the positive way forward. Some will overeat for a few minutes of enjoyment in the taste of food, others will avoid food.

Lonliness ~ Without friendships, family, and/or church and other organizations to fill our thoughts, and fill our calendar with a schedule we look forward to, lonliness is inevitable. It really walks hand in hand with isolation.

Low self-esteem ~ Dis-satisfaction with our life, whether it be our job, our marriage, our looks, or our weight, these thoughts often carry the burden of an accompanying feeling of futileness. In other words, regardless of what we want in life, or how much effort we exert, we feel that we are just going to fail one more time again. We all at some time, or another in our lives need support, encouragement and understanding. Yet rejection is more difficult for some to accept and move forward, It is as though the gears wind down and everything stops!

Again, it is suggested that those who feel burdened and weighed down seek and reach out for something in their life that provides a sense of positivity! Whether it come from professional Counseling, church and religion, music or some form of activity, it is important to take action in some form of intervention.

Waiting for someone to notice and take us by the hand is often missed. This is because we as individuals are so good at hiding our feelings, embrassed by what some might think of us. We don't need that because we are at times, our own worst enemy. Therefore, many will seek that temporary high and reach for those sweet, high fat meals that satisfy the body, and puts one in the mood for rest in order to digest a big meal. For when we are asleep, we are not dwelling on negativity. A brief escape indeed, but certainly not a repair of long standing.

Low Energy ~ This emotion is highly associated with having expended a good bit of energy, perhaps being ill, disappointed, or simply eating in excess of those food types that provide little or no nutrition. When we eat this way, or are sick we require some type of positive action. A visit to our physician to see if we are truly sick, such as an infection, or something else is going on. When we are able to realize we are not eating properly, we have the power to make a positive change in the right direction.

At this point, it is more than fair to say that negative feelings and emotions effect our health and well being, effect us emotionally, socially and spiritually. When we eat healthy, live a pro-active life, which means seeing our primary care physician as soon as we suspect something may be wrong, we are moving in a positive direction.

Positivity in and of itself *is* energy! With energy we feel we will explode if we do not get outside and ride our bike, take a walk in the park, visit family, go shopping, call a friend, but *do* something!

This type of thinking reminds me of a sort of, *Humorous type of Learning!* I once read a small piece about a huge flooding in an area where people were so flooded that they were calling out for help and receiving passage through neighbors in smalll boats.

One man climbed to the rooftop and sat there waiting for God to save him. Some offers came through people with space inviting him to climb down from his rooftop and jump on board as theirs was one of the last boats leaving the flooded area as water was rising quickly to the second floor of the homes.

When a man shouted out to the man on his rooftop again saying. "Come on, what are you waiting for?" the man answered; "God will save me."

The irony here is that God will not come down to each home and each rooftop, but when He provides a way for us to help ourselves, we should not hesitate to take that path!

Chapter Fourteen

Recommended Daily Supplements

Antioxidant

B+ Vitamins ~ The B Complex vitmins provide support for the Central nervous system, and can be helpful with such occasional issues, such as anxiety. Vitamin B-12 especially plays a vital role in nerve function and as we grow older, it is difficult for many to absorb certain vitamins. B-12 it has been learned is associated with depression and dementia when there is deficiency. **B-12 is not available from plant sources.**

Digestove Enzymes ~ Digestive enzymes with prebiotics and probiotics assist those who unknowingly have eaten small amounts of gluten, those who for whatever reason, are not making sufficient digestive enzymes. Without digesting properly, one may not be able to utilize the source of vitamins and minerals contained in their food and possibly resulting in a vitamin or mineral deficiency, digestive problems and more.

Vitamin-C ~ Vitamin C is a good source for antioxidants that help to reduce and/or make harmless free radicals, prevents the disease of Rickets and more.

Vitamin D-3 ~ Vitamin D works more like a hormone than a vitamin as much research has suggested. Those with fair skin, and those who have had cancer are usually recommended by their doctors to "stay out of the sun." In following those instructions, one can also become deficient in the "Sunshine vitamin", which is vitamin-D. Again this vitamin is often more difficult to absorb as we become older. **Vitamin D-3 and vitamin B-12 are found in meat. Also, Iron and a few other nutrients are found in meat.**

Note: Vitamins D-3 and B-12 are not found in plant protein.

Therefore, it may be a good idea to supplement if one is a Vegetarian, or possibly in the elderly.

Other Vitamins and Minerals ~ Although a On-A-Day Multi vitamin is not a bad idea to take daily, depending upon the potency, type of supplement, and possibly where it is manufactired, it may not provide all that is needed.

Magnesium ~ This Mineral is essential for healthy muscles, and prevents leg cramps, etc. It is found in green leafy vegetables, such as spinach, Kale or Mustard greens. Also available in some nuts, such as Cashews, Tuna fish, pumpkin seeds and even a bit is found in dark chocolate.

Note: Preferably purchas only supplements manufactured in the United States, and in a readily digestible form, such as a capsule.

Pills are dense and require more time and hydration to be easily digested.

Another reason to decide upon a daily digestive enzyme taken prior to your main meal.

As always, I recommend a supplement of Omega3, 6 & 9 taken probably 3 to 4 times a month.

Chapter Fifteen

What Should You Weigh?

Often times individuals find that when they are successful in losing the desired weight that they had needed to lose, they are at risk for deciding that they want to continue on losing as much weight as they can. You may even hear them say in response to a family member's comment saying "You are getting really skinny" by replying; "That is just in case I gain back some of the weight I have lost."

People who have been obese, or morbidly obese because they were obsessed with food can be at risk for continuing to be obsessed after losing weight and that can lead to another very different health issue called Anorexia. An obsession to remain focused on food, however in the opposite direction, by not eating sufficient calories to remain healthy.

That is why this Weight Loss program that I suggest to you, of course after running it by your doctor, is not about counting calories, which keeps one's focus on food.

Rather, it is about choosing healthier types of food, exercising and perhapings trying a modified Intermittent Fast. And not running to the scale everyday!

Mny charts are available for both men and women, and shows acceptable weight ranges depending upon age, height and frame. When some want to fall below that range, that may not be wise. Often, an extra five to ten pounds is absolutely acceptable. Whenever one catches the flu, or has surgery, they will often lose weight, therefore seeking to be lighter than is recommended can set one up for losing more weight during illnesses.

Below, find a few examples of average ages, heights for men and women and exactly where they should fall, allowing ranges between several pounds that compensate for age and bone structure.

The following information regarding "How much should I weigh for my height and age?" is taken from Medical News 8Brazier, Updated on June 29, 2023:

Body mass index (BMI)

Body mass index is a common tool that measures a person's weight in relation to their height.

~ A BMI of less than 18.5 suggests someone underweight.

~ A BMI between 18.5 and 24.9 suggests a healthy weight range.

~ A BMI of between 25 and 29.9 may indicate overweight.

~ A BMI of 30 or higher may indicate obesity.

However the Center for Disease Control, or CDC also notes that BMI does not assess an individual's body composition or their health. It is a screening tool that people should use alongside other tests and assessments to determine potential health risks.

BMI Calculator

According to AARP, your BMI (a ratio of your weight to your height) helps to determine if you are at a healthy weight.

Calculator available at aarp.org Or follow the Formula:

Weight (pounds) divided by Height (inches) squared, multiply by 703, and round to one decimal place.

Back to Medical News Article;

Weight and height guide chart – Using BMI tables from the National Institutes of Health.

Height	BMI Weight 19-24	Over Wt. 25-29	Obesity 30-39	Severe Obesity 40+
4ft 10 pounds	91-115	119.138	143-186	191-258
4ft 11	94-119	124-143	148-193	198-267
5ft	97-123	128-148	153-199	204-276
5ft 1	100-127	132-153	158-206	211-285
5ft 2	104-131	136-158	164-213	218-295
5ft 3	107-135	141-163	169-220	225-304
5ft 4	110-140	145-169	174-227	232-314
5ft 5	114-144	150-174	180-234	240-324

5ft 6	117-147	154-177	184-237	245-328
5ft 7	121-153	159-185	191-249	255-344
5ft 8	125-158	164-190	197-256	262-354
5ft 9	128-162	169-196	203-263	270-365
5ft 10	132-167	174-202	209-271	278-376
5ft 11	136-172	179-208	215-279	286-386
6ft	140-177	184-213	221-287	294-397
6ft 1	144-182	189-219	227-295	302-408
6ft 2	148-186	194-225	233-303	311-420
6ft 3	152-192	200-232	240-311	319-431
6ft 4	156-197	205-238	246-320	328-443

BMI ~ Age is not a factor in BMI for adults, but it is for children. This is because children typically grow larger with age. The CDC use both age and sex assigned at birth in its BMI calculations for people between the ages of 2-19 years. The Center for Disease Control, CDC charts use percentiles that compare measurements with boys and girls of the same age and gender.

Some of the problems with BMI is that it is provided only as a basic measurement, while it takes height and weight into consideration, it does not account for factors such as;

Waist or hip measurements

The proportion of distribution of fat

The proportion of muscle mass

These factors can affect health. For example, high performance athletes tend to have a lot of muscle and little body fat. They can have a high BMI because they have more muscle mass, this does not mean they weigh too much for their height.

Another limitation of BMI is that it does not distinguish between people of different racial or ethnic groups. Studies have shown that non-Hispanic white, non-Hispanic Black, and Mexican Americans may have significantly different levels of body fat but the same BMI as people from other groups.

This inaccuracy may lead to disdiagnosis or an incorrect assessment of risk factors between individuals.

BMI can offer a rough idea of whether or not a person is at moderate weight, and it is useful for measuring trends in population studies.

However, it should not be the only measure an individual uses to assess whether their weight is ideal.

Another measure is the <u>WHR</u>, waist size with that of their hips. A high WHR has an association with higher levels of visceral fat, the fat in the bdominal cavity that surrounds several major organs.

For this reason, the WHR can be a useful tool for understanding potential health risks when considered alongside other assessments of health.

A 2018 meta-analysis suggests that having a high WHR can put people at a higher risk of myocardial infarction, or heart attack.

Measuring WHR

To calculate their WHR, a person should measure around their waist at the narrowest part, usually above the belly button. They can then divide this measurement by the width of their hip at its widest part.

For example, if a person's waost is 28 inches and their hips are 36 inches, they will divide 28 X 36, giving a WHR of 0.77.

What does it mean?

Using WHR, a World Health Organization (WHO) report defines abdominal obesity as follows:

In males: WHR of over 0.9

In females: WHR of over 0.85

However, as with BMI, the WHR does have limitations. For example, this measure does not account for a person's total fat percentage or their muscle-to-fat ratio accurately.

Optimal WHR differs based on sex assigned at birth as well as race and ethnicity, according to the 2008 World Health Organization (WHO).